THE HOME SERIES OF GREAT MASTERS

For Piano

Frédéric François Chopin

© 1993 International Music Publications Limited
Southend Road, Woodford Green,
Essex IG8 8HN, England.

NOCTURNE IN G MINOR.

Op.15, No. 3.

CHOPIN

NOCTURNE IN E FLAT.

Op. 9, No. 2.

CHOPIN.

ÉCOSSAISE IN D.

CHOPIN.

NOCTURNE.

Op. 37.

CHOPIN

Andante sostenuto.

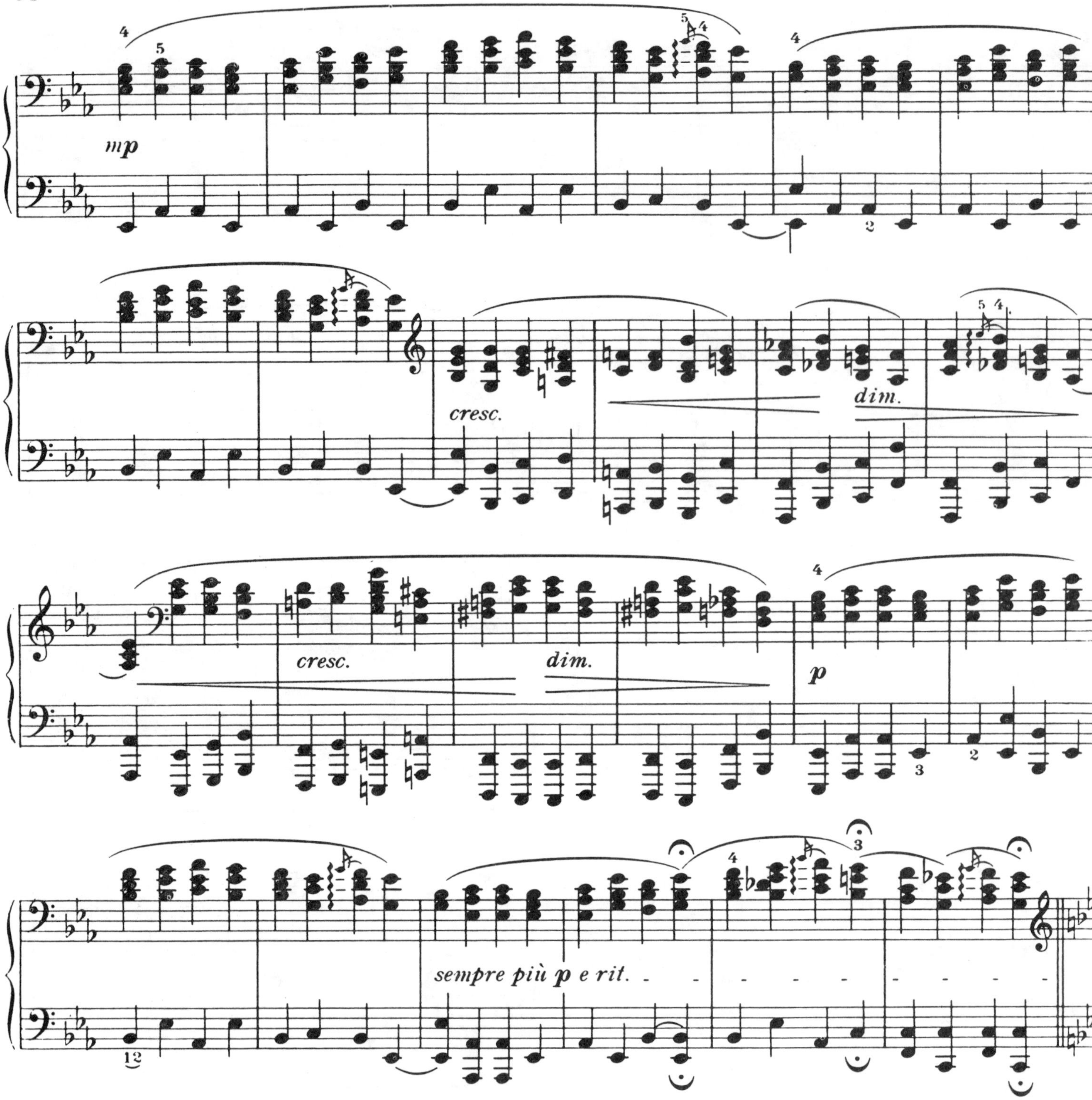
mp
cresc.
dim.
cresc.
dim.
p
sempre più p e rit.
pp
p
Ped.
Ped.

WALTZ.

Op. 64, No. 2.

CHOPIN.

Più lento.

dolce

poco rit.

WALTZ.

Op. 69, No. 1.

CHOPIN.

Tempo I.

MAZURKA.

Op. 7, No. 2.

CHOPIN.

Vivo, ma non troppo.

D.C. al Fine.

MAZURKA.

Op.17, No.2.

CHOPIN.

Lento ma non troppo.

8.

MAZURKA.

Op. 33, No. 1.

CHOPIN.

MAZURKA

Op. 41, No. 2.

CHOPIN.

MAZURKA.

Op. 59, No. 2.

CHOPIN.

11.

PRELUDE.

Op. 28, No. 6.

Lento assai

CHOPIN.

12.

POLONAISE.

Op. 26, No. 1.

CHOPIN.

Allego appassionato

PRELUDE.

Op. 28, No. 15.

CHOPIN.

MARCHE FUNEBRE.

CHOPIN.

15.

ANDANTINO.

from Ballade in F. Op. 38.

CHOPIN.

LITHUANIAN SONG.

CHOPIN.

MAIDEN'S FANCY.

(SONG.)

CHOPIN.

18.

Un poco meno allegro.

Printed in England by Commercial Colour Press, London E7